Both Sides
from the
Middle

Poems by Star Coulbrooke

Printed in the United States of America

Publication by Helicon West Press

Cover art: Jane Catlin
Book design: Maria Williams

ISBN: 978-0-9977444-2-2
First Edition

To my Mitch,
without whom none of these poems would exist.

Contents

Both Sides
from the
Middle

Education of an Idaho Farmgirl

Into her mind of two story clapboard
corner bedroom, braided rug, chenille bedspread

window unscreened, frog-croaking chorus
like doors open-groaning rusted-out hinges

into her skin, grit under ivory
bangs cut straight across forehead

past pirouette aqua-net tutu
black tap shoes, runner-skates

into white-cold sunstroke hills with cows
demon migraine fainting spells

white chalk screech on black slate
ladders to the apricots

hot car swerved to semi's headlights
flip and roll overturn onto crushed roof
hospital bed, bloody insides, bottle of aspirin

into the principal's office, nurse's office
admissions office, college gates

she has come this far she has left the cows
the fields the barn the breeze freshing-in

she walks glasslike thin gold lettering
book-spined burnished she is turning away

from across the pasture off the river
down the sloping hills the river canyons
groaning whistling calling her back

she can't go down that road again
she's saying to herself I knew you then but oh
I know you better now

I

Fringe

I sit at the crooked desk
in the adult-education classroom,
mesmerized by the purple fringe
at the wrists of my blouse sleeves,
watching it drag across my notebook
as I write, the way it might have
if I'd worn this blouse years ago
in the high school homeroom
where I penned his name
over and over and inserted *Mrs*
in front of it, as if it were something
I could magically become
at only fourteen, the thing every girl
I knew imagined in the innocence
of pre-connubial bliss, a new name
scrawled across her future
like embroidery on trousseau.

Summer Notebook

The summer I was forty I hiked myself
right out of a marriage, its chasms
and insurmountable rocky ledges,
decades of fear, no fight left in me,
only flight from coiled springs of timid need.

The summer after my divorce I wandered
the desert hunting rocks and lizards with my lover
and had a nervous breakdown working at a nursing home
where scorpions nestled in diaper boxes
and patients fell out of their chairs waiting for me
as I hurried like I do in bad dreams, the faster
I run, the more I can't get where I'm going.

The summer my daughter was five she played
the wear-your-clothes-backward game
in her say-the-opposite-of-what-you-mean club,
donned cast-off hats and mismatched shoes,
hid them in shrubs on the corner before
she caught the bus to school. A visiting artist
called her up on stage to sketch her, embarrassing
her older sister and making me think of freedom,
of what it would cost to be as impetuous as a five-year-old.

Living Alone

I

Dime-thin cracks
invite the mice
to squeeze
their bony frames inside.

Cat, wild
with listening, waits
for that small gray
seeker of warmth.

II

A quick embrace,
one teasing lick,
then the grip
that stuns to submission.

In this game,
cat only wins
if mouse
comes out to play.

Bears

I

I'm not making this up
about the two of them

The wife's already checked
the garage for his truck

gassed and buffed
for the hunt

guns polished and blued
in the rack

whiskey bought
ready for a fight

Anything
can set him off

dusty mantle
crumpled rug

a tool out of place
even the look on her face

II

Along their stark expanse
of vinyl six feet high

two black iron
silhouettes

noses facing north
legs at a lope

Plodding head bent
past the bear decor

the wife wipes her feet
at the porch

and opens their front door
with sleeved hand

not to mark the brass
with fingerprints

Someone Else's Now

There sits the seventies brick rambler
with the rose-peach gable ends
and triple stack chimney,
the brick she picked out
with her spouse, now her ex,
the paint she insisted on mixing herself
to get the color no one else
in the valley had seen or achieved,
so their house was set-apart.

It was set apart, lawn immaculate,
trees placed for perfect shade, brought
from her mother's place
for free, considered for weeks
before digging the hole. She dug the holes,
hauled the new saplings,
watered them to stately canopies.
Then she left them, left that perfection
of house and garden, the garden she built
with elliptical walls, planted with yucca
and iris, pansies and four-o'clocks.

There sits the side-yard
where she scraped the mounded earth
from left-over clay and rock,
heaped it up with topsoil,
planted its borders in bright orange
marigolds and filled the inside with dark

purple petunias, a contrast
that startled her neighbors.

They were the neighbors
who scorned her after she left,
believing the opposite of why,
their only view on the outside.

There it stands, run-down, re-painted,
re-faded after years of other families,
no longer that rosy hue, that envied façade,
floors swept and re-swept
of the eggshells strewn in every room
in the house she built and made exact
and left to someone else.

Permanent

Twenty-one years since the new hairdo,
since she whacked off the curls
cascading down her neck. Instead,
short spikes, tossed every which way.

Just in case, she saved the perm rods,
three sizes, with 3X3 papers
and flip-over elastic keepers. Saved them
in a plastic cosmetic bag, eighties-style,
foil mirror, White Linen, Lash-Flash.

Also in the bag, a box of powder
too dark for her complexion, twenty-one years
of hats and sunscreen, no more worshipping
the deep tanned hide of youth. Hard mistakes
bound for the second-hand store.

How odd, she thinks, the things we save.
How strange to note
the permanence of shedding our own skins.

Aerobics by God

It was a class for women-only,
women in the same church
honing their bodies for husbands
who told them God said
it was good to be fit,
and ever since birth control,
women could be.

So every Tuesday morning
they followed a church-approved leader
through ladylike routines
in new leotards and ballet shoes,
embarrassed at the sight of butts
and legs they'd never seen before,
their shapes always having been covered
in Sunday pleats and gathers.

Gradually, as confidence crept in
with dance steps mastered
to such easy routine they could have
walked it in their sleep, their thoughts
began to wander, endorphins
they hadn't owned since puberty
pushing them into loving their muscles,
liking their new form—such energy!

A few of the ladies quit, went off
to the fitness center in town
and started working out with weights.

They bought cross-training shoes,
aerobics and lifting on alternate days.
Made excuses for not going out with
the family on weekends, went running
on Saturdays, hot-tubbing Sunday.

They were looking sharp, feeling
like they could conquer the world.
One ran for public office, two divorced.
I burned up a new pair of shoes
every six months, got so tight and sinewy
I stopped my cycle, no more monthly
bleeding, just energy, energy and power.
I could carry six bags of groceries
to the car myself, no cart, no sweat.

I could stay up until midnight baking,
doing laundry, cleaning the bathroom.
I'd fall into bed, sleep hard until five,
get up and go like hell. One day,
my man voiced his usual complaints,
and I decked him. All from a church-ladies
gentle aerobics class, ordered by God.

Thongs

Had a pair of pink thongs.
Little girls are supposed to like things
pastel and floppy, toes out in the open.
I liked the slip-slopping sound
of rubber hitting pavement,
slapping back up against my feet
like a birthday spanking.

Some of us never outgrow our lust
for the plunge of a strap on skin,
the down and up of dampish rubber
whapping our senses into summer,
sweaty flesh bathed in that tingle of want,
more than want, a palpable need.

Tattoo

Brittle parchment:
Thin as faded fly-wings,
ruined skin pulls off
with the tug of a sweaty sock.

Underneath:
Colors vivid as sex,
symbols harbored in ink,
attitude seven layers deep.

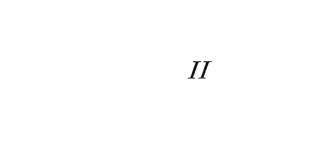

II

Rock Chucks, Birds, and Lizards

I once knew a city rock chuck
who lived in the parking lot
at the heavy equipment rental,
North Main Street, Logan, Utah.
He played in the front loaders,
under back hoes and tractors,
popped up out of the asphalt,
it seemed, when I parked
in the driveway on Sundays
when no one else was around.

On our farm, before I was born,
my sisters had pet rock chucks
who came down from the hills
to live under the front porch,
but Mother said they were dirty
little things and she was glad
when they finally died out.

In the small town where I spent
my married life, there was a bird,
I don't remember what kind,
but it lived in our neighborhood
for a season and dive-bombed
my daughter every day
for a week. It flew out of nowhere
and pecked at her head
when she walked up the street,
same place every time,

halfway between our house
and the high school. At fifteen,
my daughter vowed to drop out
if I didn't drive her there,
only one block away.

Hiking once in Southern Utah,
I met a lizard on the West Rim Trail
in Zion National Park. It caught
a grasshopper half its own size
and slowly ate it, head-first.
Banged its own head on a rock,
back and forth, back and forth,
to knock the hopper down its throat.
I watched the wings disappear,
and when the jagged hind legs
were all that stuck out, the lizard
massaged its throat on a rock
and swallowed hard.

In a Saint George oil and lube shop,
my partner and I watched a displaced
whiptail climb the cinder block wall
while we waited for my car.
The owner said, *Hey Ralph,*
bring out the lizard catcher,
and Ralph came out armed with a can
of carburetor cleaner, hit the lizard
with a burst of spray, and it dropped,
dazed, in the parking lot.
We do it all the time, they said.

It scares the ladies
when it climbs the walls like that.

And we took the whiptail home
with us, built it a big wood and glass
aquarium with a bed of red sand
and a hot rock, and we fed it
crickets and mealworms, because
I remembered the time I sprayed
my trees for tent caterpillars
and found a dozen dead birds
on the ground around my Chinese elm
the next day, remembered how
I used to spray my yard
for bugs and weeds bare-armed
and bare-faced, and I thought,
sometimes we're simply afraid
of the wrong things.

A Woman Reconciles Herself to Living With a Quota of Animals

Inside her eight hundred square feet
with two dogs, two cats, and a man,
the woman ponders another adoption.

But every morning it is already a contest
for her lap, of which there is only one,
and every one of them is too big for it.

And every time she comes home they are
waiting in a bunch, wagging, purring,
kissing her on the mouth, wanting dinner.

And they clutter: dog toys, fake mice,
shirts, newspapers, hair balls, which she must
pick up before bedtime or she cannot rest.

The house is barely big enough for six,
she realizes as they cluster around, her kitchen
an obstacle course, five sets of eyes all on her.

The Artist and the Carpenter

I'm painting the bathroom.
He chose red.
I should be studying,
but instead,
on pine bead-board, oak
cabinet,
I've been spreading thick,
deep red.

I stand on the bathtub edge
to get at the stiles
that run up the cupboard,
rails that cross
next to the ceiling,
rosettes for the corners.
I run my paintbrush
down curved channels,
lay soft bristle over ridges,
follow the lines he drew up.

Red gets in my eyes.
It washes down porcelain
fixtures, seeps into vertical
wainscot joints
and pools in tiny clots
on the new wood floor.

I clean it up with rags and
razor blades

but faint traces of red remain,
and later I see thick
red drips,
hangers, he calls them,
dried on the perfect grooves
of his eye-level stiles.

Red pendants.
They rest on smooth contours
of plinth blocks
he cut, planed and sanded,
installed at the base
of the cupboard.

Red jewels.
Deep red.
Fresh blood, ripe fruit.

Hangers dancing in sunlight
streaming through the window
falling on a work of art,
a double work of art,
and I go back to my books,
satisfied.

Along for the Ride

Fear of death.
Fear of living too long.
Fear of death.
        I've said that.
                —Raymond Carver

Friday evening, waiting
in somebody's driveway, dogs
barking in the back of the car,
dinner baking in the oven
at home, everything on hold
for this weekend because
I don't know if the man
I'm waiting for will ever
come out of that house.

And I could sit here
until neighbors call the police
when they hear gunshots,
and they might come and tie off
the property with yellow
DO NOT CROSS POLICE LINE tape.

They wouldn't let me leave.
I'd have to make a statement
and then the ambulance
would arrive and they'd
haul him away, and since

we're not married or related
they wouldn't let me ride along.

I'd have to fill out forms
and they'd finally send me home
after they rounded up the killers.
I'd sit there alone with our dogs,
crying, waiting for a phone call
from his family. The minutes
would drag by like hours,
and when they finally called
to say he was dead, I would
never leave my house again.
Except to go buy dog food.

And I would eventually
waste away, though right now
I feel like I have enough
fat stores to last for a long
time, but I guess it only takes
a month or so for starvation
to set in, and they'd come
and take me to the hospital
and my dogs would have to go
live with my sister.

The house would be paid for
by the insurance company, but
it would sit vacant until
I was well again, and my job

would be waiting, maybe,
and I'd come home every night
and knock around by myself,
too sad to write.

I'd be so lonely I'd have to
take long walks in the hills
with my dogs to keep from
going crazy again, because
I wouldn't want them to get
shuffled around every time
they put me away.

I'd start to get eccentric,
and people would talk.
I'd imagine him still living with me.
We'd have coffee together
every day at 7 AM and 5 PM.

We'd sit at the kitchen table,
our dogs lying underfoot,
make plans for the future
and talk about all the fun
we used to have together.

We'd kid around and bash religion,
and I would tell him about
my students or my day at the museum
or whatever about wherever
I was working.

We'd go to bed together
and hold hands all night.
He would soothe my worries
about the violent world we live in,
the anachronicity of death
and the nature of love.

Got Eight Hours

Sometimes I just want
a good thing to go on
and on.

Having resolved
the question of sleep
I reflect on rest,
distant cousin of repose,
kin to slumber–

Daydreams encouraged.

Wander, alight, observe,
move only when the body
says ready.

Won't answer the phone

unless I'm compelled

to stretch out

my voice box,

put the receiver
against my ear, say hello.

Leaf through a magazine.

Iron a couple of butterflies
on my ink-stained shirt sleeves,
as long as it doesn't
violate my lazy day.

Go to bed early.

Perhaps,
          rested enough,
                    I'll retrieve
those dreams that
          disappeared

                    years ago
when someone in charge
handed down the decree
against sleep,

hyped up our workday
to nights and weekends.

Pliant, the unrested,
          prone to suggestion.

Whatever happened
to hanging around
in a bathrobe,
spending an entire

afternoon in a hammock
slung between trees
near a river,
no wireless feeding tube?

Dreams can be deferred
interminably.

But that doesn't mean
I can't get them back.

Refreshed by sleep,
reveling in lavish indolence,

I aim to throw a wrench
In the deprivation machine

And find the rest
of my life.

Disconnected Cell Phone Blues

It feels like the last thread broken, he says,
between me and my son, the canceled cell phone
we've paid for since he was eighteen
and now he's twenty-nine. We've decided
to stop the family plan, ease our budget crisis.
Besides, my stepson says the only calls
he makes are to his wife when he'll be late,
never calls his dad who now feels bereft,
as if his son hadn't left home years ago.

I've come in from my evening walk,
first line of a poem on my mind,
something I need to write down right now,
but he's playing Kenny Wayne's "Blue on Black,"
telling me his lifeline's broken, as if he can't pick up
the phone and call his son's landline any time,
as if paying for his cell phone is our only tie.

Meanwhile, I've lost the muse, the line I had
in my head, something about the moon,
my words and the mood turned off with the stereo,
though his tune still moves through my head,
along with his dejection, his closing the CD case,
placing it on the shelf, and slowly shuffling
through the kitchen to the shower, to silently
drown his sorrow in a stream of hot water.

Next week I'll be cooking for six, playing dolls
with his grandkids while he and his son talk business,

when his son's wife will mention moon-cycles
over a sinkful of dishes, and I'll remember
the lines I didn't write because he had the blues,
the broken-thread blues, as if his family ties
would be severed with the cell phone we disconnected,
as if wireless signals were as irretrievable as the line
I lost tonight between here and the full, silent moon.

Men Working

They have ulterior motives,
the worker I live with admits.
And I almost enjoy
the insinuation of sex
into my mundane middle age,
apprised of men's pleasure
in flexing their bodies.

I see them on rooftops
of the tallest buildings in town,
some in hats and flannel,
faces lined from years of sun,
the younger ones oblivious
to heights and U.V. danger,
bare-chested, muscles rippling,
heat-bronzed, pants tight
over hard butts and thighs.

I watch them in my front yard
on bobcats and back hoes
scraping out the worn driveway,
pouring new cement, workers
with triceps like knotted cedar,
hormones thrusting, confident
my eyes are on them, on the one
who strides across my lawn,
hoists a three-gallon cooler
to his shoulder like a whiskey jug,
bottom to his lips, and presses

the dispenser. Water streams
into his mouth and mine.

Excavation

We found the first minuscule bone structure
in the crawl space one winter when the plumbing froze.
It looked like a salamander skeleton, fragile
bone cage, long pointed tail, triangular jaw.
Torch-lit, the spidery ghost held our imagination
until pipes thawed, then we tucked it away
in a dresser drawer, trove of recovered trinkets.

No one can say why realization descends when
it does, but this year, in the early stages of
renovation, we pried the kitchen floor up
and there in powdery black dirt, undisturbed
for decades, lay an entire community of dead,
and we knew the skeletons were mice, knew
the one we had forgotten in our bureau drawer
was at least a distant relative, unfortunate souls
who met their death by freezing or poison.

But more intriguing than the mice, who squeeze
themselves flat and get in before you can blink,
was the desiccated cat body we found
sealed inside our back porch landing, lying
among pork chop bones and tin can lids.
On its side, legs outstretched (like my cats when
they're full), it looked illogically content, as if
it had gone happily to sleep and forgot to wake up.

We bent to pick it up—the bottom half was gone,
nothing left but the stench we must have imagined:

Surely a cat so long dead wouldn't smell bad,
dried as it was. Perhaps we felt guilt for the cat
surrounded in its tomb by remnants of food,
for the mouse whose bones we misidentified and set aside
until all those mice who died for lack of warmth
came forth, like the cat, and prompted recognition.

The folklore of ancient builders might claim
well-fed cats buried under houses are a boon
to those who walk above them, a talisman for peace.
We hope for a good omen with this cat, fur dissolved,
skin dried to a leathery carapace, one eye a hole
that seems to look right through us—a mystery
we don't want to solve, afraid for the dawning
of mouse bones on our paltry human conscience.

III

Cooking Before the Frost

"Into the red/Eye, the cauldron of morning"
Sylvia Plath, "Ariel"

"Red sky at dawning, sailors take warning."
Folk-Saying

Rain pours hard as knitting needles
down from a black April night,
cruelest of spring storms, killing frost
on its surly heels, no pity for the apricots.

I stir egg yolks and white sugar for lemon
pudding, wait for bubbling thickness
to cook into clarity, milky starch
glossed to a sheen we eat with spoons.

Rain suddenly stops. We know what this means
for tomorrow's prickly fate, red sky
too beautiful for any good to come of it,
bird bath frozen solid, finches dropped
from bitter perches, blossoms black
on every tree that blooms this cursed month.

I must use the whites before they spoil
so I beat them, foam to peaks. Add sugar,
vinegar, vanilla, sweet, sour, sweet
or the stiffness won't hold when put to heat.

43

Dark clouds roll in again like chocolate
folded into egg whites, puffed
meringue at the end of baking, bitter
sweet mouthfuls of shadow and air.

Shrug

Cloud shoulders press
hot rain through sun's bright sash,
colors spreading prismatic,
mounded landforms greening-up
against a backdrop of faraway.

This semi-arid ecosystem
too much to imagine, almost magic,
this climate, this transition zone.

Weather splits, muscling
hard against the middle, El Nino
fanning its troops, thrusting
marchers en masse to the castle,
onslaught of rain then sleet
until at last the sunstream breaks
and birds come out to bathe.

Here in the city, skyscrapers mirror
desert and tropics oppositely,
sidewalks drowning in the aftermath.

A gilded patterning like gold leaf
glints off slanted rooftops,
apology for all of us huddling here
in sodden spring, wondering
what it means, the shrug, the wink.

Lift

Hummingbirds hunker
in moss-lined nests,
babies barely hatched,
lightning flashing
brilliant through the canopy.

Family dog won't settle,
restless in high pressure
building through the afternoon.
First lash of light across her eyes
she leaps on the bed
and burrows like a vole.

Eight hours of storm later,
we rise to ponder the day,
what will happen
to the outdoor wedding,
everything ready, poised
at the edge of weather.

Hummers have already lifted
cool and damp in sunrise air,
wings flickering like filament.

Rise

White-shrouded commute
except where fog lifts,
mute wisps from the valley's
narrow slipper.

Halfway up surrounding
mountains, barren
branches slant west, bowing
to cemetery's precipice.

Wind-blown from canyons,
storm systems airlift
over the pressure-lock.

Down in the valley, particles
too fine to filter, a clot
in the lungs, two years
off your life. Up there, breath.

Yellow Yarrow

Yellow to gold from June through August, taupe in September,
Embers on umbels atop strawlike stalks gone spotted with mold,
Last of the summer's fickle weather.
Long days give way to sun red with smoke,
Old rituals of burning fields at harvest-end, the yarrow a border
Wanton and stubborn along the wire fenceline, hardy as cactus.

Yards and yards of yarrow-hedge, wide, profuse, sturdy
As the tech-industrial building glinting in slick siding
Rising just across the highway to the West,
Reflecting morning sun, sheen of steel and glass,
Omen at the start and end of every season,
Woven in the landscape, summer in the seeds, and fall.

Valley Fever

What is a valley
without blue mountains
rising in the distance
or brown mountains up close,
mapley clefts darkening
as the sun dips, tan mountains
like Buddhas rounded
and creased,
swelling above the flats
where traffic
zips along smooth highways,
quadruple stripes
of speeding headlights
entering the wide plain
where golden windows
gleam on sloping hillsides.

What is a valley
without its bustling people,
without spacious barns
and cows lowing in the fields,
pigeons wheeling
from church steeples,
song birds trilling down
at feral cats below the feeders,
where the family dog
wheezes and stumbles
from sniffing up fungus,
damp and drought

creating disease
which smothers dogs
in a matter of days.

Does the fever exist
despite or because of
the people?
What is this fever
if not a burning-off
like fires that blaze pines
in summer,
brilliant explosions
we line up on sidewalks
to watch
from the safety of town,
looking to mountains
of glittering ash,
black as a sky of stars,
each one its own answer.

Power Lines

We turn our eyes to progress, to helicopters, cabled nets
slung beneath their bellies cradling monster erector sets,
T-frames a hundred feet high, latticed and riveted,
cross-bars jutting like elbows, set down
in upright pose, a ballet on one toe.

Dozens of these dancers
take their stance on the swath,
once an impasse of granite,
maple, aspen and pine,
now a dance floor highway-wide
extending for hundreds of miles,
power buzzing through the wires.

We ascend, years-long drought
padding the trail in flour-fine dust.
Above us, the vibrating air surges,
prickles our skin with invisible sparks.

Thrumming in symmetry, steel frames dance
En Pointe across the distance as far as we
can see. Under massive girders, we urge
the stunted maples to defy those
choreographers of clear-cut,
machines that chew up
mountainsides to quell
the threat of fire.

We dare the wires to snap, to fall
in graceful arcs from the arms
of their dancers, swirling
and sparking, a pirouette
across the skyline,
a final flaming
revolt.

Highway to Migraine

Sheets of purple oil fan out
over pavement, tires roll
no stopping, take the corner
sliding steel to steel until the car
makes that leap into thinness

Halt in midair with halos,
ocean waves, plumed birds,
red comets golden edged

Rush of light and color lasting
only seconds before the descent

Press of landing stopped
in a vise, brains a fat raccoon
under the roller your skull
a thousand pounds of constant
bearing down, you move
with the impact into days of
grinding pain, and then it lifts,
a passing-through to light
and tallness, the world going by

Desert Birds at Dusk

What do these small birds know
about roads, about cars?
They flit past our windshield
from the nowhere of sky,
fading one-dimensional
with the darkening horizon.

What do these swallow-like birds
think of headlights, their wingflaps
like mothwings? Moths fly toward light
while these birds veer just in time,
joyful belly-dive deflected heavenward.

How might they magnify sight
to catch the movement of a mayfly hatch
down a hollow three plateaus distant?

What else do they know flying over
the desert at dusk? We can't pin them
by color or wingbeat, identify
their species in the fast-falling dark.

Back home, we stare at waxwings
landing in the bare-limbed Snow Crab,
visitors we easily identify each year,
these birds we think we know.

Letting Go

Every day the deer stop by, tip the narrow
squirrel-proof feeders into their mouths
and guzzle then chew, a leisurely grinding
of slender jaws, flat teeth, ears straight up
and those big brown eyes staring us down
where we stand behind the glass and watch
as if we're in the zoo and they have paid
their admission. Fences don't hold them,
nor walls if the door is left open.

Hours into the daily storm, sleet sheeting
straight down on snow-drifted walkways
cleared and re-cleared then buried,
deer tracks in fours to the fenceline,
fifty-pound slabs of ice shunting off
the steel roof—we've turned the radio off
indefinitely, no inside noise to blunt
the weather, break the next bad news.

What can it hurt? What if they jostle
until the tan siding buckles, windows
wide to the coming spring and the dogs
joyous, racing down the brick path?
Feeders refilled, the birds flock in as if
yesterday's hawk didn't snatch a lesser
goldfinch off the slender hawthorn limb
on which they rub and rub their beaks
to break the hard seeds open.

Keep the radio off. What happens next
will be night or morning, sleet or snow,
deer in the yard not under the eaves
saving themselves from starving,
rain on the roof where slabs of ice
form boulder-size, crack and let go.

Housebound

Ice needles the metal roof,
pierces plaster ceiling designs,
frosts the newly-painted drywall.
So cold our nose hairs break.

We bow our heads, an avalanche
scrubs us raw. We say to each other,
We've got to get out of here,
knowing we're not going anywhere.

Going nowhere takes resolve.
Takes knowing. How to apply
peanut butter to un-gum a sweater,
separate burrs from long hair.

Meanwhile, we strap on skates,
glide across icy floors to stanch
the stab-wounds in our plaster,
frost falling like dandruff.

IV

Solstice Kitchen

I stand alone in the kitchen
washing dishes from solstice dinner,
their smooth round heat
all that remains of children visiting,
children who were once a size that fit inside
the sink beside me as I worked,
and now their own children
are too big for sink-sitting.

Outside the moon shines over
the frozen earth where states away
a baby was born to a child of mine,
a child who once toiled
in the kitchen over broccoli,
instructed to start dinner while I gardened.

I placed the cutting of florets from stems
in her little-girl hands, and she,
not knowing, cut each tiny bud away,
pieces too small for the strainer.

She cried there in the kitchen
while I worked in the sun, longest day of summer,
coming in at last to see broccoli stems
lined up on the drainboard
and a thousand green seeds floating
in the sink like miniature water lilies.

Caesarean

"For more than a millennium, the survival of the Gypsies has depended on secrecy: on disguise and misrepresentation, on keeping customs and ambitions hidden, on burying the past."

Among the Gypsies, Isabel Fonseca

I

6 A.M. surgery prep:
  My daughter, her husband both
  vanish past the doors of
  No admittance of children under fourteen
  without special permission.

Grandbaby Dee and I
  wait. Her brother,
  little Kip Elijah, is coming out today.

Star, that's what she calls me,
  the peck-bird is coming
  to the hospital too.
  It has to peck Mom's belly-button
  to get the baby out.

Dee is a Gypsy. Her mom is my daughter,
  her dad a Romichelle. Not sure how
  to spell it, neither is he. Their
  language is oral, not written.

They are a traveling family
> stopping over to have a baby,
> lending their Gypsy lore to
> the place they're in at the moment.

Back to the peck-bird, the Labor and Delivery
> doors. We wait, cartoons on TV,
> *The New Yorker*, powdered donuts
> and cranberry juice for an hour.

But Dee doesn't follow hospital rules.
> Gypsy children don't conform to
> No Admittance. We go in
> the double doors, demand to see her mom.
> They let us.

All my life, if I had only spoken,
> made the demand, I could have been
> admitted. Instead, I was quiet,
> dreamed of running away with the Gypsies.

II

This is Utah. *In Mormon culture,*
> Terry Tempest Williams writes,
> *authority is respected, obedience is*
> *revered, independent thinking is not.*

For years, she sat in hospital
> waiting rooms, obeyed the signs of
> No Admittance, watched the women in
> her family die.

For her, the price of obedience
        came too high. Now she questions
        everything, openly defies *No Admittance*
        Beyond This Point.

She travels with her friends
        to the Nevada Test Site
        to take back the desert in the names
        of their children.

They walk across the cattle guard from
        BLM land, are immediately arrested,
        thrown into holding pens, and
        trucked out on a bus.

III

My daughter said, when Dee was a baby,
        I've met a man. He's good to me.
        There are things I can't tell you.

When a Gypsy marries a gadje,
        my daughter, a person outside
        the tribe, there is a promise,
        an allegiance to be made.

For weeks, I wouldn't hear from them.
        Dee learns new words, but not
        a new language. The language is fading.

Ultrasound and television,
        delivery rooms and snack machines,

tax and license, health insurance,
proof of identification,

trailer courts that charge as much as
apartments, work that can't be found,
a wife whose babies don't descend,

family scattered from Kansas
to Texas, Florida to Wisconsin
dilute the Gypsy life.

The new father, slender, straight
black hair, almond eyes,
bends down with Dee's little brother.

IV

In Wisconsin
in the woods
Gypsy children played.

At dinnertime
a car horn sounded
twice, kids swarmed
into the camp from
every direction.

Doesn't happen these days,
he says. Now there is
too much crime.
Too many murders.

No matter where they travel, danger.
        In KFC in Logan, small-town Utah,
        they watched a gun fall out
        of a customer's coat and clatter
        to the floor. At a rest stop
        in Colorado, a tall dark man
        stood between Dee and her mom,
        blocking the rest room door.

They live at gas stations.
        Dee knows no woods
        but she plays at city parks
        in every town.

V

They come home
        from the hospital a day early,
        settle in with their new baby.

She smells plastic burning,
        he hears buzzing in the fuse box
        in the bedroom.

Get out, get out, he yells,
        flying out the back door
        of their trailer.

She lands in the snow,
        bare feet, baby in one arm,
        Dee in the other,

staples torn, blood soaking
her nightgown.

He kicks at the electrical plug,
          frees it from the hook-up post,
          grabs an extinguisher.

Black and thick, smoke rolls out
          the fuse box into the bedroom.

The what-ifs, later, are phenomenal.
          Seven minutes, start to finish,
          in a trailer fire.

VI

All this bravado:
          I distance myself so my
          children can't hurt me.

Get close, they may tell me too much.
          They hurt out loud, and I
          catch the pain.

The pain comes inside if I listen.
          If it does, I can't help it.
          Can't help them.

So I put on a brave front,
          an aloofness, don't worry.

Distance and coolness, that's
        how I get through a life
        with children.

VII

Later, I hear they are leaving
        again. Last fight she had
        with Dee's former dad, he threatened
        to burn them alive.

A Gypsy man protects
        his family. His woman stays
        home. Their home is the camp.

1985, Ficowski: *Opposition*
        to the traveling of Gypsy craftsmen
        began gradually to bring about
        the disappearance of traditional
        Gypsy skills.

Not enough work around here,
        they say. In twelve more years,
        the baby will be a man.

Well-proportioned, straight
        black hair, dark eyes, strong
        and smart: a Gypsy, like his sister Dee.

VIII

They'll go to California.
    His cousin wired some money,
    says there's work down there.

I went to California once,
    mid-sixties, fifteen,
    rode with Hell's Angels.

Yearning for the Gypsy life,
    I told my daughters this,
    but really I went in a Chevrolet

with two guys. One had an original
    Hell's Angels jacket. We picked up
    a hitchhiker, skinny old man who

climbed in the back seat, lit up
    a smoke, thanked us for the ride,
    tried to start a conversation.

My friend in front, the driver,
    sat up tall, rolled his shoulders,
    adjusted his leather jacket to show

Hell's Angels stitched on the back.
    The old man stopped, mid-sentence.
    Hard enough life to worry about

getting rolled, let alone end up
        murdered by two Hell's Angels
        and their girlfriend.

IX

We drive into the camp,
        their trailer is gone. A gaping hole,
        a pulled tooth, a space of gravel ground
        between two curbs. Electrical post devoid
        of plugs, block of wood kicked out
        from under a tire, the tire, the wheel,
        the trailer, gone.

In the middle of the night—
        that's the best time to drive.
        You eat up road as far as your
        headlights go, thousands of miles,
        millions. The cool, the radio,
        your woman beside you, your
        home behind you, that's
        the way to travel.

X

In the old days parents told their
        naughty children, If you don't
        be good we'll sell you to the Gypsies
        and you'll never see us again.

Folklore advertises fear.
       Tragic stories, oldest slander.
       Private lifestyle, hidden language,
       different moral boundaries,
       world view codified.

The fear is racism. The fear is
       that of Hitler for the Jews,
       of McCarthy for Communists.
       The fear is hate for difference.

They are a separate people,
       a lost tribe, lost because
       the time is not yet right for them.
       Their lies are not the thieves' cant,
       but survival.

XI

Got a letter from my sister yesterday.
       You baby boomers, she said,

seem not so much moved
       by democratic ideals as the need
       to assess the total morality

of our planet. You blame us
       for our use of deadly poisons
       and atomic energy.

You've seen the effects of acting
*   without sufficient*
*   information.*

My daughter, the one
        who isn't a Gypsy,
        wrote a theme paper
        on nuclear testing.

She gathered information,
        assessed the situation of our planet,
        crossed the line at the Nevada
        test site with TTW and friends.

Now she tells me
        sometimes she wishes
        she could travel with her sister,
        forget about all of it.

XII

In the 1950s, Gypsies didn't live in
        Utah, but they were Downwinders
        like the rest of us. Wherever they

traveled, they couldn't escape
        the American nuclear mistake. Each test,
        162 of them, Chernobyl ten times over.

Government deception, Carole Gallagher says.
        Good, gentle people victimized,
        toxic secrets hidden in the landscape.

Mormon hierarchy officially silent,
      politically in charge, its people
      obedient, faithful, patriotic.

Babies died, mothers got breast cancer.
      Clusters of leukemia deaths in 1951.
      Radiation sickness diagnosed neurosis.

A thousand scientists issued a warning
      in the mid-fifties about health effects,
      small demonstrations began. But when

Darlene Phillips wanted to join them
      she asked her Bishop what was the proper
      role for a good Mormon woman to take,

he said, *No, you stay away from it,*
      those people are communists. So she
      didn't go. And Ground Zero kept up

its nuclear numbing, *A natural byproduct*
      of trauma tangling our wasted, bloodless
      bodies in shock waves of betrayal.

XIII

Poems of the gypsies,
      1950s, weighted with
      fatalism:

The long road, the
          rootlessness, no
          turning back,

the poverty, illiteracy,
          lost dreams and
          impossible love,

the no place of home,
          nostalgia of doom:
          Let it come,
          it doesn't matter.

XIV

Evening news, January 15:
          In Topeka, Kansas,
          they're creatively recycling
          missile silos, remnants
          of the Cold War.

One sold, forty thousand dollars,
          to a bookish couple.
          Two-story library, modern
          kitchen, greenhouse.

The old control panel
          decorates one wall, the other,
          a bricked-in missile exit
          adapted to an entry door.

One silo a high school art lab,
    new school house built on top.
    Saved the taxpayers
    six hundred thousand
    construction dollars.

It cost four million dollars
    to build the silos. The school
    gets, for one dollar, their own
    18-inch-thick concrete walls
    and a drive-in bus garage.

XV

They called from Kansas
    last year, tornado warnings
    on TV in every McDonald's,
    every gas station,

black funnels taller than
    outer space, able to pick up
    trailers like pieces of paper.
    Came back through town
    on their way to Florida,

checked into the clinic
    with an ectopic pregnancy,
    lost one fallopian tube. Just
    as well, it was hurricane season
    by then.

Earthquakes in California,
       but that's nothing next to
       tornados in Kansas. Missile silos
       won't save Gypsies
       who don't live there,

like bomb shelters wouldn't have
       saved us baby boomers, but we
       didn't know it. Gypsies at least
       know their own fate.

Song for a Daughter Thirty Days Clean

In the midst of her returning,
you can feel the spreading stillness
where anguish wracked your breast,
this moment of her spoken love
worth the twenty years it took her
to discover how you waited, why
you waited, while she moved
through life like wet cement.

Before the gray sludge hardened
into forms she could not break,
she somehow softened, became pliant,
putty in her own hands, to shape
a new world she might yet inhabit.

She widens her landscape, invites
your voice, asks you to sing her
back home. The brilliance of sunset
rings with reprieve, no hard glare
of morning clanging its gong, not yet,
just this stillness, this peace, this
brush stroke of luck. This simple,
grateful moment, holding its breath.

An Old House and Two People

I

We saw the house for the first time
three summers ago on a drive in Idaho.

Interested in different things, we
vacationed together on weekends and

semester breaks in between his
drywall jobs and my term papers.

We left the freeway at the Malad
River Valley, took the old road

along miles of abandoned dryfarms.
He dreams of renovation, restoration,

houses and lots of land. I want a
quiet room near a college library.

II

We came into Malad City by the back way,
farmland ending at a few tall grain elevators,

abandoned houses all over town. He took
pictures of porches, railings, gable ornaments,

patterns for the old-style new home he wants to
build some day, and then we saw it. The house.

It stood on a large corner lot in the center of
town, set back from the street, concealed by trees.

A forest of Chinese Elm bordered the lot, enclosed
the house. Box Elders leaned on the roof, lilacs

canopied the sidewalk, plum trees nestled next to
the porch, vines grew up the red brick walls.

III

He figured the house to be late 1800s, a two-story
hall-and-parlor, its upkeep neglected for decades.

We followed the sidewalk, ducked in to the forest of
foliage dark with shade, walked up to the front door.

It was wide open. Inside, we waded through piles of
newspaper, magazines, cardboard, clothing and bedding.

Carpet corners showed underneath stacks of garbage.
Sun-faded easy chairs molted, shedding their stuffing,

letters and documents drifted out of a roll-top desk.
A legless double bed propped up on Books of Knowledge

trailed yellowed sheets and dirty blankets on the floor,
and a dead cat spilled maggots onto the faded bed spread.

IV

We picked our way over paper sacks full of socks and
underwear, fallen plaster, boxes of rusted food cans.

He said, *I'd give anything to have this house.* We went
upstairs, narrow banistered steps, hall, three bedrooms.

*I'll make the east room your office, line the walls with
bookshelves, put your computer desk next to the window.*

The south room will be his workshop, the north one a
bath with a walk-in closet. Back downstairs, he already

imagines the kitchen he'll build, sees through the junk
knee-deep on the floor, the wood stove layered in grease.

Plans the new cupboards, pantry and breakfast nook,
an east-facing bay window for our mornings together.

V

Three years later, the house is ours. Trees lie in
tangles, downed branches all over the yard, where

city fire crews promise to burn them for a drill. Faded cedar
and asphalt shingles wait in piles to be hauled to the landfill.

Inside, lath and plaster fall on sheets of old wallpaper
covering half-rotted carpets left to serve as dropcloths.

Truckloads of household furnishings, ruined, have gone
to the dump, the man who owned them dead thirteen years.

Lost his mind long before then. He lived alone, missing his
dead wife, hiding in his house, reading his books and letters.

He confined himself to their bedroom, covered the windows, lined
the walls with blankets and cardboard and sacks of socks, and died.

VI

This morning we take four-by-eight sheets of plywood
off the truck and carry them into the empty front room.

We'll start with the roof, now he's ripped off the
shingles and bolstered the beams with hurricane ties.

Last week he hooked the rotted front porch to his truck,
pulled it off the front of the house. He'll rebuild it, he says,

along with the missing porch on the other side of the house,
the one that left its ghost on the old red brick. And my eyes

wander over the littered yard, and I think of how many years
it will take him to finish this project, and I wonder about

noisy neighbors and whether my room will ever be finished,
and how I always seem to live inside somebody else's dreams.

Sunni Cleans the Fridge

In case she dies on her next trip
        (car crash, gunshot,
        slipped
        in the motel bathtub),

Sunni makes sure he'll start out
        fresh, nothing on the shelves
        to grieve.

He'll miss her like an arrow
        buried in the neck
        of the bled-out deer
        he could never locate.

When they moved from his place,
        they tossed frozen steaks
        from second-storey windows
        to the guard dog in the dirt yard,
        icy meat clunking his black head
        as he wolfed packages whole.

No freezer-burned meat in this house,
        no moldy bacon.
        In the morning
        she'll toast him
        an English muffin
        with cheese.
        No moldy cheese.

Waffles can stay, his morning ritual:
      freezer, microwave, toaster,
      onto the table with all his pills
      and imitation maple syrup.
      Spray-on butter substitute.

Sunni thinks maybe tonight, with the milk,
      a tapioca pudding. Even grief
      won't keep him out of that,
      especially with Cool Whip.

She could stock the freezer for millennia
        with Cool Whip alone.
        It never goes bad,
        like Twinkies, one symbol
        away from chemical.

Cooked pudding will use-up the last eggs,
      cookies already baked,
      not his favorite. She'll take
      them to work, give them away.

The apples, too, and the cucumbers.
        Tomatoes she picked to save
        from the frost. She walked
        the neighborhood, saw tarps
        and blankets spread on gardens.

Not hers. She figures, let it go. He'll never
      miss it, like he'll never
      turn the compost, never

mow the lawn again, pick up
dog poop. Why bother
if she's gone, his motivation.

Sunni wipes the glass shelves,
leaves the jams in their jars,
pasta in boxes, flour and cereal,
essentials she'll need if she comes home.

It could happen. Ever since
she learned to drive,
she's imagined her demise,
a semi crossing the yellow line
and she's the deer in its headlights,
so she cleans the fridge in case she dies,
but every time, so far, she hasn't.

Empty fridge can go two ways:
Nothing for him to throw if she's gone;
Texas Roadhouse otherwise.

Sunni Looks Up

Sawdust builds, piles up
in hills through the house.
She sweeps and sweeps, no
dust pan, no collection bin
for his collections, for
what's left of him: carpentry,
reams of music, guitars
he strummed now sunk
in the swim of what she must
give, throw, or drown in.

Sweeping, she's dreaming
his carvings, his fishing lures turned
on a lathe, old men with hat brims
turned down, sea birds fastened
to willow twigs. Dreaming of storms
in his old-time magazines,
waves crashing shore where women
in finery hold up their dress-hems
and men in dark business suits step
into sand, water washing their shoes.
Imagines them page after page
yellowed and curled, lifting like wisps
on her broom, adrift to where clouds
amass, black, boiling blue.

She is always looking up, sky a marker
for the way she feels day into night,
her self not just hers but reflection of his,

moon shining over the remnants he keeps
of earth's quirky skin, tree bark and burls,
nature he shapes into carved limb and orifice.
Sees herself everywhere, faces of others,
crook of a tree, cliff ledge with pigeons.
Valleys and dales of rivers eroding with age
as their world fades to dust and she sweeps,
coffin wheels tracking through bristle marks.

No Comparison

My pain, he says, is worse than yours,
mine's magnified a thousand times, I'm
sure of it, the worst pain you could ever
feel, worst pain I've had in my whole life.

>*I recall the pulse of raw nerves,*
>*how the signal travels*
>*like power conducted through jelly,*
>*how we live with such pain.*

They should cut my arm off, it hurts
so bad, knowing, as he says it, they won't.
Limb gone, the pain would only register
same place it used to be, causing agony.

>*How do we measure it,*
>*how shall we say ours was*
>*worse, when it's over, a*
>*ghost we barely believe in.*

Harvest

On the kitchen counter
jars of pickles, dill with peppers,
peppers with vegetables
suspended in vinegar, sharp tang
masking (barely) the smell of cod
fillets broiled for dinner.
Husband is yearning
for longer life,
his cancer returning.

Wife lets him help
with canning.

He stirs fat peppers
snapping and smoking
in the pan, a slick of canola oil,
skins pierced, juice burning his eyes.

She cuts long strips of carrot,
red bell peppers. She peels onions,
he peels garlic.
They stand side-by-side, industrious
after dark, holding the news
inside, each thought a texture
of its own, the color of future.

Whose life will be set-aside first,
his, with its bright varied snap,
or hers, its vinegared spark?

Who's to say which will be preserved
and which will be tossed
like the skins and gratings
of all they've peeled-back,
brightest colors pressed into jars,
shelved, shining.

Repurpose

To retire on disability is to admit
the Stage 4 Cancer, so he gives away
his boy scout jamboree collection,
gives away his drywall tools, marbles,
clothes he'll never wear again—but not
his bandsaw and gouges, acrylics and brushes,
not the glass he finds in the garden,
broken bottles, shattered dishes
glinting in the soil, polished like the sea.

He plans next year's planting, builds
climbing-bean structures from cattle fencing
and metal stakes, tacks one-by-twos at the edges
where sharp points snag his shirtsleeves.
Glass and rocks and purslane strew
the ground where he pounds the posts.

He imagines a shop where his glass
will inlay the grips of walking sticks,
where his carvings will bring
exorbitant fees if he gives away
coffee (shade-grown, bird-friendly).

He'll have a ceramics guild, an art gallery,
a book shop. He'll crush glass in a contraption
he invents and make a million dollars.
He'll mix Italian sodas in his biker-bar.
In his Church of Blues, he'll play guitar,
serve greens from his garden, kaleidoscopes
placed at the tables turning his mosaics.

Sun Catcher

Glass panels gently tap
the window pane
in blue red yellow orange
fishing-lined together,
diamond shapes and beads
between.

They bounce
on gusts of wind
blown down
from snow-topped
mountains
east of town.

Brilliant crafter
who thought
to throw the sun
against an inner wall
as wind's relentless
mangle
sets its geometrics
tapping,
stops the death
of birds
who in their nesting season
try to fly inside
what's mirrored.

Now they veer instead,
no more crashing
into glass reflecting
what's outside, not in.

Sun catcher, hung to tap
the golden light and flash
its colors like an ambulance,
a therapy, colored glass
in a stiff breeze.

Two Sides of the Road: A Walking Tour

On the hillside to our left, evening primrose
blooms ghost-white among short milkweed,
spike-leaved, clustered with tight yellow buds.

On our right, a golden deer. It claims the yard
where this house once made-up the neighborhood,
no others but the deer, four more appearing
among swing-set, playhouse, dark green lawn,
ears twitching, grazing as we walk on by.

Look left again above our newfound primrose
to houses hunkering like giants, plaster facades
grinning down the gravel delta, wooden stakes
and orange ribbons marking subdivisions
yet to join them, families with children waiting.

See the deer? They cross this road twice
every day, new obstacles to jump with every phase
of moon we'll soon see rising on the right
like half a lemon in the sky, salted with profiles
of backhoes, dump trucks, mortgage-makers.

Take heart for the swallows that dip and tumble
through the bug-thick dusk, gorging on mosquitoes
that whine past our ears as we swat at them,
as the peach-pink sunset spans both sides of the sky
and closes to steel gray clouds, yellow half-moon
haloing the grazing deer, burnishing the primrose.
And you, seeing both sides from the middle.

Acknowledgments

Grateful acknowledgment is made to the editors of the following publications in which these works or earlier versions of them previously appeared:

Black Rock and Sage: "Got Eight Hours"
Crab Creek Review: "The Artist and the Carpenter"
Creosote: "Highway to Migraine," "No Comparison"
Hunger Magazine: "Along for the Ride"
Petroglyph: "Rock Chucks, Birds, and Lizards"
Pilgrimage Magazine: "Excavation"
Quill and Parchment: "Solstice Kitchen," "Song for a Daughter Thirty Days Clean"
Red Owl: "A Woman Reconciles Herself to Living with a Quota of Animals"
Soundings East: "Tattoo"
Sugar House Review: "Cooking Before the Frost"

"Aerobics by God" appears in *Logan Canyon Blend*, Blue Scarab Press, Pocatello, Idaho, 2003, and in Perspectives, Center for Women and Gender online magazine, Utah State University, Spring 2015; "Men Working" appears in *New Poets of the American West*, Lowell Jaeger Ed., Kalispell MT, 2010; "Thongs" appears in *Logan Canyon Blend*, Blue Scarab Press, Pocatello, Idaho, 2003; "Harvest," "Repurpose," and "Sun Catcher" appear in *The Helicon West Anthology: A Ten-Year Celebration of Featured Readers*, Helicon West Press, Logan, Utah, 2016.

My sincere gratitude to Shanan Ballam, Brock Dethier, LeeAnn Gilbert, Helen Cannon, Jane Catlin, Nancy Takacs, Maria Williams, past and present members of my poetry group, former and current students and colleagues in the USU English department, and all who have supported me in my role as Logan City Poet Laureate. Thank you for your belief in my work, for the insight you share, and for the inspiration I draw from your words.

The internationally recognized poet, May Swenson (1913–1989), was born and raised in Logan. Proceeds from this book will go toward a fundraising effort to build "The Swenson House" and gardens on the original family plot, as a tribute to May, a vibrant literary venue for the community, and a destination for May Swenson-inspired poets and fans from all over the world.

About the Author

Star Coulbrooke, Poet Laureate of Logan City Utah, is co-founder and coordinator of Helicon West, a bi-monthly open reading series that publishes community broadsides featuring poetry, prose, and visual arts. The series released its first collection of prose and poetry, *The Helicon West Anthology, A Ten-Year Celebration of Featured Readers*, in 2016. Star also founded and coordinates Poetry at Three, a local writing group in its twenty-fifth year. Poetry at Three gives April Poetry Month readings with a sampler-collection of new work each year.

Star's poems are published internationally in literary journals, magazines, and anthologies. She co-authored a chapbook, *Logan Canyon Blend* (Blue Scarab Press, 2003), with Kenneth W. Brewer, the late former poet laureate of Utah. Her chapbook, *Walking the Bear* (Outlaw Artists Press 2011), is a tribute to the Bear River in southeast Idaho and is available online at the University of Utah's Marriott Library. Her most recent poetry collection, *Thin Spines of Memory*, was released in 2017 from Helicon West Press.

As Logan City Poet Laureate, Star conducts monthly poetry walkabouts and poetry workshops, from which she composes collaborative community poems using lines contributed by those who attend her events. She presents a new collaborative poem to the City Council each August, with her last poem to be delivered when her five-year term ends in August 2019. Star also composes poems for various events and public figures, one of which was her poem for the inauguration of Utah State University president Noelle Cockett in May of 2015.

At Utah State University since 1992 as student, employee, and faculty member, Star has served as USU Writing Center Director since 2008. She oversees a staff of 60-75 tutors at five writing centers and collaborates with faculty from across the curriculum to create better writers. She is a long-time activist for rivers, public lands, wildlife, domestic animals, and humans. Star lives in Smithfield with her artist/carpenter/musician partner Mitch Butterfield and their labby-heelerish dog Chezley.

Photo by Marissa Lords Devey